How to craft time and make money

100 techniques on how to earn with free invested time

Debra P. Mcdonnell

About book

This digital book was written to provide information on Web advertising. Every effort has been taken to make this digital book as accurate and full as is reasonably possible. However, there may be mistakes in the text or typography. Similar to that, this digital book only provides information up to the distribution date. This digital book should therefore only be used as a supplement and not as a primary source.

This digital book is intended to instruct. This digital book's author and distributor make no claims that the information is accurate and disclaim all responsibility for any errors or omissions.

Time, they say, is cash.

If that is the situation, this brings back the way that certain individuals are unquestionably getting significantly more cash in a similar measure of time you will place in, or even at an extensively far lesser time.

At this point, you have likely derived the way that there must be a superior method for playing the lucrative game.

Indeed. There are 100 different better ways of playing the game.

It is feasible to procure more by working less. You've seen others make it happen. Now is the ideal time to compose your example of overcoming adversity and get it going in your life. While expanding your efficiency will give you two times as much return, finding a better method for playing the game will potentially bring you multiple times or more returns.

Additional Time, More Cash

1 Get familiar with the lucrative capability of subsidiary projects.

This is one well-known and exceptionally successful method for procuring recurring, automated revenue, which is gotten from setting up a site that pre-sells organization items. In this arrangement, the organization gives the items along the programming code that tracks down deals, of which you will be given a commission for each effective deal. Find organizations that are referred to offer greater commissions as well as track down clients who are almost certain to make different buys overstretched timeframe, which will produce repeating commissions.

2 Make data items like digital books.

The web gives an extraordinary method for making and selling a digital book that makes sense of "How To" data, for example, How to Begin Your Internet-based Business, or some other subject intended to give data on the most proficient method to make life simpler for individuals. There is a gigantic interest in data, which is something you can profit from. The incredible thing with digital books is it's simpler to make, and you can finish in a short sum of time. Once finished, you need to concoct a site, secure a web facilitating administration and set up your web-based promoting setup. This will make it feasible for your digital books accessible for buy 24 hours every day, for a considerable length of time to come, with the chance of procuring pay while you rest.

3 Procure uninvolved remaining pay through publicizing commissions.

On the off chance that you own a site or you are wanting to possess one, work on drawing in guests or creating web traffic by giving significant, unique, and new

4 Become an affiliate of web facilitating administrations or space enlistment.

Offer web facilitating administration wherein you pay a month-to-month expense and exchange the help at a specific membership charge to your clients. In any case, assuming you are wanting to take part in this kind of administration, it is essential to be completely comfortable and learned with the web facilitating administration to offer brief and dependable help to your clients.

5 Become amazing at pay discussion.

During new employee screenings, rather than trusting that the compensation discussion will be handled, you can feel free to ask the questioner/selection representative the normal compensation of the position you are applying for. This way you don't need to sit around going this way with discussions since you definitely know the figures and can choose quite a bit early if it's something reasonable enough for you to seek after your application.

6 Keep your messages short and brief.

Rather than going through valuable minutes forming long and winding messages, keep everything short and direct. Your headline, right off the bat, ought to be educational so your beneficiaries will be aware assuming it is something they need to focus on. While immediately passing on your message, make a point to try not to build sentences in latent voice.

7 Get business and prospective customers effectively by straightforwardly inquiring.

individuals on the off chance that they have an issue you can help resolve.

For instance, if you are offering website architecture administrations, rather than looking at assuming there are individuals keen on having another site, pose direct inquiries, for example, "Who among you isn't content with their ongoing site?" This successfully chops down the pursuit and you get to save a huge measure of opportunity with regards to getting reactions.

8 With regards to working with a group, more often than not 80% precise is sufficient.

As you probably are aware, time is cash and more often than not huge undertakings have time limitations. On the off chance that you are working with a group, it is quite often sufficient to accomplish 80% precision. You can leave the leftover 20% for the rehearsing or testing stage, where you can iron out the better subtleties. Remember that taking care of business properly and on time is more vital than getting every one of the subtleties right.

9 Converse with a human client care delegate.

While calling client care, rather than conversing with a computerized machine, get quicker and more proficient goals and backing by going directly to a genuine individual. If you have a significant or earnest grievance, attempt to check contacthelp.com or gethuman.com assuming there is a code for the particular organization you want to call, and sidestep the robotized frameworks.

10 Become amazing at saying "No."

Before genuinely committing any responsibilities, assess your ongoing responsibility and regard your cutoff points. Figuring out how to say no won't just save you time except will likewise save you from a great deal of pressure. Effective individuals understand what they need and experience with no difficulty being definitive, putting their foot down on something, and saying no.

11. Gain proficiency with the specialty of appointment.

Assuming you are the sort of individual used to doing everything all alone or you experience issues of giving up, remember that you need more hours in the day to do and take care of everything. This is a vital worth each supervisor and pioneer ought to learn and acknowledge. Decrease your responsibility and upgrade proficiency by figuring out how to assign errands.

12 Review to get preparing for a particular expertise.

Nowadays, a profoundly attractive and specific range of abilities can move you from being only a standard representative to a more important one. Find the opportunity to figure out what are the most important and sought-after abilities in your industry and check to assume it is something that you can figure out how to get during your extra time.

13 Procure a higher capability or degree.

There are sure work areas that require having a specific degree, particular preparation, or testament to qualify you to a more significant salary scale. While this course might be monetarily testing and tedious, it can build your capabilities and make you qualified for advancements or higher assignments, which can end up being a decent and compensating interest.

the long run. Whether it's an MBA degree or a Six Sigma Dark Belt, look at the off chance that going through night classes and courses can end up being possible speculations. There are

 likewise, organizations that support further instruction for qualified workers, so find the opportunity to talk about this with your organization's Human Asset Office.

14 Think about changing your work hours or working from home.

On the off chance that your manager can't or is reluctant to give you a compensation raise in remuneration of how much work you do, attempt to arrange to change your work hours or examine working from home choices. Be that as it may, this may not work for various enterprises but rather on the off chance that you can finish the vast majority of your work from home, then, at that point, it's most certainly worth inquiring. You can likewise assess your work hours and check if chipping away at another shift can help your efficiency or open up additional opportunities to seek after other lucrative open doors.

15 As opposed to filling in as a full-clock, consider turning into an expert.

If you are continually working far more than the normal 40-hour work week, you might need to investigate functioning as an hourly specialist, assuming it is more plausible monetarily. While this may not mean you work any less, this offers you more adaptable work hours, accordingly permitting you to take on extra clients and acquire additional pay as opposed to working all day and not getting extra time pay.

16 Interest a compensation raise if you are accomplishing more or contributing essentially.

If you believe you merit a raise for how much benefit you are getting to your organization or you are accomplishing more work than you are initially recruited to do, by all means, request a raise in light of your presentation. You can time your

demand for a raise after an exhibition survey. On the off chance that you end up being an incredible resource for the organization, the administration wouldn't fret about paying you more to hold your administration.

17 Track down an effective approach to doing monotonous assignments.

If your work or everyday undertakings expect you to take care of monotonous errands on a normal premise, rather than investing a lot of energy finishing them, attempt to sort out how you can mechanize or smooth out the whole cycle. There are a ton of online applications and programming items online intended to chop down the bare essential stuff. Utilize free applications, which can fundamentally chop down how much opportunity to get done with a specific job. Assuming you feel now is the ideal time to buy paid programming, carry this up with the administration and try to come outfitted with motivations to legitimize the cost. Generally, this product can help in altogether expanding efficiency, and exactness and give simple admittance to coordinated data.

18 Consider changing position or making a strong professional move.

On the off chance that you feel your profession is confronting an impasse and there is no open door to change into a fulfilling and better balance between serious and fun activities with your present place of employment, think about investigating better open doors. Find another workplace where your experience and abilities are enormously esteemed. The primary concern here is, assuming you are exhausted and come up short on, it's time you take care of business.

19 Consider taking on an independent composing position.

If you have an energy for composing or have a strong handle on good punctuation, correspondence, and spelling, you might need to look for open doors for independent composing position. You can contribute articles to magazines, papers, and other neighborhood periodicals to procure additional pay. Progressively assemble your portfolio and work in your direction towards laying out validity.

20 Show a language.

Do you be aware and communicate in another dialect? Or on the other hand, perhaps you have solid order of the English language to qualify you to educate it. This is a popular ability that can open up extraordinarily lucrative open doors.

21 Perform Web research occupations.

Assuming that you are certain that you feel comfortable around the web, you can offer your expertise as an internet-based scientist to neighborhood organizations.

22 Become a "green" expert.

Individuals are excited about making way of life changes that can result in involving less energy in their home. This is an immense industry that can assist you with making critical money by assessing homes and making suggestions on the most proficient method to turn into "green". Over the long run, you can likewise offer your administrations to organizations.

23 Sell natural produce.

Assuming that you love planting and know natural strategies, think about selling natural produce. Contingent upon exactly how huge your gather is, you can offer "in season" natural vegetables as well as new spices to cafés. Culinary experts are continuously watching out for providers that offer the best and the freshest.

24 Sell collectibles and one-of-a-kind pieces on eBay.

On the off chance that you have great information on collectibles, go through your ends of the week exploring among secondhand shops and carport deals as well as swap meets where you can

possibly score old, significant fortunes at little to no cost. Lead somewhat of exploration and sell it off on eBay.

25 Get compensated to shop.

Various organizations employ individuals to perform what is known as "secret shopping" and report their encounters to companies. While participating in this kind of work, you want to make a point to be fair and you have a decent handle and comprehension of the business.

26 Brighten cakes.

Assuming you love to prepare, bring in cash as an afterthought making and enlivening cakes. Flaunt your baking ability and propose to heat cakes as well as different treats to neighborhood office break rooms, little bistros, nearby stores, and so forth.

27 Make and sell sticks and jams.

If you know how to can and save sticks and jams the old design way, you can make a huge clump and sell sticks and jams that are in season. You can either decide to sell it among companions and partners, to a nearby market, or much over the Web.

28 Bring in cash out of your photographs.

On the off chance that you own an extravagant camera and you have a style for taking staggering photographs, set out to utilize it by offering your administrations to unique occasions like weddings, parties, and corporate capabilities. You can likewise present them on web-based locales and bring in cash each time somebody chooses to download and utilize it.

29 Set aside some margin to figure out your investment funds.

To bring in more cash, you want to ensure all your reserve funds are striving to procure benefits. Assuming that you have a singular amount of cash that you are ready to take care of for around a year or longer then get a fixed-rate account.

30 Take in a guest.

While the vast majority spend a fortune to claim a home, what about causing your home to procure and create its benefit? If you have an extra room, think about leasing it out and procuring additional pay as an afterthought.

31 Lease a vehicle parking spot.

Assuming you are living near the downtown area, or close to a football arena or train station, and you have a carport or parking spot that you don't precisely utilize, it's a supposed goldmine directly in front of you. Lease your parking spot to suburbanites or show/game occasion fans and bring in additional cash as an afterthought.

32 Sell on eBay.

You understand what they say regarding one man's trash can ending up being another man's fortune. Assuming you have such a large number of unused belongings that are taking up long-lasting residency in your cellar and squeezing your home, then, at that point, consider unloading pieces on eBay and bringing in cash.

33 Response paid overviews.

There are various internet-based overviews accessible where you will be compensated for your viewpoints, either through remuneration vouchers or money.

34 Proposition virtual help administrations.

With a developing number of electronic organizations today, virtual help administrations are currently exceptionally popular. A ton of organizations and individuals utilize the administration of virtual help to lead explores, perform tedious positions, find things and settle on telephone decisions, and so on.

35 Bring in cash by facilitating a web-based discussion.

Programming, for example, SebFlipper can have various separate discussions under a solitary server. You can bring in cash by charging discussion administrators or proprietors for your facilitating administration. You can likewise offer this assistance free of charge and post your promotions and standards on their gatherings to create pay.

36 Do podcasting.

This is like a video or voice contributing to a blog where you can discuss a few fascinating points and bring in cash from the promotions show. If you have a gift for jabber, and you believe you can give pertinent data or fascinating feelings, you can contact many endorsers through this stage.

37 Arrangement your day ahead and stick to it.

Assuming you have to give arranging a shot at your day and expect the potential road obstructions, you will observe that you are more ready to handle difficulties and divert issues with no sweat. This will assist with guaranteeing you will have a more useful day.

38 Separate your huge plans into more reasonable achievements.

Attempt to accomplish something beneficial consistently. Assuming that you plan out your objectives and set timetables and courses of events, you have more inspiration not to relax or stall.

39 Beginning your day by handling first the more troublesome and the tedious undertakings.

Here you have full energy to go through all that before steadily continuing toward simpler ones.

40 Figure out how to best manage breaks in a definitive and self-assured way.

Try not to permit the insignificant worries of others to occupy you from your motivation. This doesn't be guaranteed to mean you should be impolite and hostile. All things being equal, figure out how to be firm and focus on significant things rather than continually winding up and obliging others' interests.

41 Quit tarrying.

Train yourself to abstain from nothing to stressing or hesitating, which just builds your ineffectiveness. Keep in mind, time is cash. On the off chance that you are continually incapacitated with stress, plan your 'stress time' toward the finish of every day so you can keep on track to handle extraordinary work and more significant worries.

42 Deal with your messiness.

Ensure everything is in its legitimate spot, this will save you time from continually looking for lost things. A clean work area can essentially assist with upgrading efficiency.

43 Adhere to your needs.

Try not to start dropping or putting off things you can achieve today. While one could say, you have sufficient time tomorrow, it's one more day to look at an entirely different arrangement of difficulties.

44 Figure out how to bunch process.

Bundle every one of the little and humble assignments that are not significant. Rather than going back and forth going to little things generally for the day, which just hinder and occupy you from additional significant undertakings, group or cluster them together and go through them each set in turn. You can make a rundown of the little undertaking and with just an hour or so left in your work day, begin handling these errands as fast as could be expected, and check every oddball in your rundown.

45 Earthy colored sack it.

While making and carrying your lunch to work isn't precisely extraordinary, it saves you superfluous cost, let us lose a greater amount of your time by managing lunch, and gives you better control of what you eat.

46 Interpretation of high-profile projects.

On the off chance that you are continually dealing with the sidelines, doing less significant things, your achievements will positively not make you a star, nor will they benefit you. All things being equal, attempt to chip in for greater tasks, the very ones that will cut your

 name and carry acknowledgment to the organization. On the off chance that you have the skill and certainty however there is an absence of beneficial undertakings, consider concocting your own. If you get along admirably, these enormous and high-profile undertakings can have a tremendous effect on your profession and life. These are the achievements that can upgrade your portfolio.

47 Bank your compensation raise.

On the off chance that you were at last given a raise, don't promptly go into considering ways how to spend your additional cash. Try not to build your consumption. All things considered, think about placing the whole sum in the bank.

48 Cautiously arrange your records and work area.

While they say innovative personalities can figure out their tumult, it can likewise add to the pressure and hamper your efficiency. Name your organizers appropriately and toss out papers and reports that can be disposed of.

49 Clean your daily agenda.

If your plan for the day is something like a mile long, go through everyone and figure out which ones are pointless. Foster the propensity for disposing of superfluous stuff and figure out how to improve your life.
50 Dispose of interruptions.
Kill every one of the superfluous interruptions, for example, IM and email alarms, Twitter, and other long-range informal communication locales. If conceivable, you ought to consider switching off the Web, truth be told. You can likewise wear earphones so you won't be occupied with standard office commotion.

51 Hold gatherings to 30 minutes or less.

One of the most well-known and greatest time-squanderers are gatherings that could be handily achieved with a call or an email. If conceivable, ask out of gatherings, or on the other hand assuming you make major decisions, dispose of them if it's not fundamentally significant.

52 Just attempt to browse your email on more than one occasion per day.

Try not to continually go through your messages generally for the day. Distribute an opportunity to go through your mail toward the beginning of your day and inquire an hour before you leave. Assuming you continue to send insignificant messages, you are making significant interruptions to beneficiaries and influencing the efficiency of everybody, including yourself.

53 When at home, switch off your TV.

One of the best ways of saving you both time and cash is to observe less TV. This gives you additional opportunity to deal with additional significant things or look for a seriously remunerating side interest as opposed to observing every one of those responsibilities instigating promotions.

**54 Go over your assortment and look at which ones
you can get freed and sell.**

Turn a basic eye and decide whether there are copies or things that you will sell. While you are busy, what about considering chopping down the time you spend on your leisure activity and searching for additional productive endeavors? You should have a lucrative side interest or procure accomplishing something you are enthusiastic about. Who can say for sure, that this could open up a ton of extraordinary open doors for you?

**55 Practice the 30-day rule while pondering making a
buy.**

On the off chance that you are enticed to go a little overboard or indulge yourself with a most recent device hang tight for 30 days and inquire as to whether you truly need the thing. Frequently, the urge will die and you wind up saving yourself a lot of cash by pausing and not following up without really thinking. It is critical to prepare yourself to get rid of the unimportant and superfluous buys and get a good deal on truly sound ventures.

56 Abstain from spending a lot on engaging your kids.

Rather than giving in to the enticement of purchasing your kid the most recent computer game or the coolest device to raise a ruckus around town, center around sharpening his imagination and value straightforward and invigorating games. Guardians genuinely should understand that youngsters don't require extravagant contraptions to keep them blissful, but rather gain incredible experiences by investing more energy with them, making stuff, and finding new things. You will find these choices less expensive and fulfilling.

57 Contact your charge card organization then request a rate decrease.

Pick any of your cards that are conveying an equilibrium and hit up the organization number at the back part. Haggle for an interesting decrease or you will mull over taking your business somewhere else. If the individual you converse with can not oblige your solicitation, then, at that point, request the boss. At the point when you consider it, if you have $5, 000 worth of offset with a 3% decrease rate, you might save $150 consistently.

58 Take care of your business.

Go through your closet and spotlight on disposing of a portion of the stuff. You can sort out a yard deal or give it to get an expense decrease. All the old stuff that is simply staying there can place more cash into your pocket. It could likewise mean opening up more storage room space.

59 Pick term extra security.

Many individuals accept that protection is speculation. It isn't. Change to term protection rather then you can utilize the distinction of the expense to settle a portion of your obligations or begin your reserve funds. Entire and widespread arrangements are essentially more costly. You are certainly in an ideal situation getting yourself in the clear financially as opposed to spending extra on below-average speculations.

60 While purchasing a vehicle, go for eco-friendliness and dependability.

Rather than going for what's well known or flashier, picking an additional eco-friendly and solid vehicle will save you a great many dollars over the long haul. For instance, while driving a vehicle for 80, 000 miles, picking a 25-mile-per-gallon vehicle more than a 15-mile-per-gallon will mean 2, 133 gallons of gas. So assuming that a gallon costs $3, that is a surprising $ 6, 400 investment fund not too far off.

Furthermore, unwavering quality can likewise deliver incredible profits, so investigate as needs be. Your endeavors will pay off for you, no doubt.

61 Abstain from going to malls and stores only for amusement.

Reveling in the need to window shop will just urge you to spend more cash on stuff that you don't require. All things considered, look for different spots to

engage you, like the historical center, the recreation area, or a companion's home. Try not to substitute shopping as a type of diversion and you will be in an ideal situation.

62 Arrangement to contribute to a private company and use a plan of action.

that has a lot of capabilities of making you rich.
If you have not sorted it out, business people start a new business since they have long acknowledged dealing with regular work won't make them rich. Be that as it may, starting a new business requires cautious preparation so try to consider every contingency. Begin with a strong plan of action. On the off chance that you can't see yourself rounding up thousands or millions of dollars with your business thought, you might need to investigate more prospects.

63 Cautiously distinguish and disconnect your center assets then choose to expand on them.

Find something you appreciate, this is a strength that you might construct and contribute on. On the off chance that you go into a business, it is ideal to wander into something that will permit you to communicate your assets then you can foster it more through redundancy. Many individuals have effectively received extraordinary monetary benefits following this course. Look at it if you can capitalize on yours.

64 Decide to work in an industry with popularity and huge net revenue.

You create gain in light of the distinction between how many deals you make and how much cash you keep from each deal in the wake of deducting the expense of getting it done or administration. If you appreciate the more noteworthy room for error, you will require

a less measure of deals to procure 1,000,000. Before getting into any business, work out first the conceivable edge of the items or administration you decide to sell.

65 Select to utilize cash.

Rather than continually charging your buys shockingly or check cards, decide to pay in real money rather for every one of those non-charge spendings like gas, eating out, and some food. Why? Paying in real money makes the experience of expenditure all the more genuine. There is additionally the way that in deciding to spend cash, you have better control of your costs as opposed to winding up spending more than you acquire.

66 Make a few negligible week-by-week investment funds move.

Attempt to deduct a couple of dollars off your discretionary cash flow consistently. You can begin by moving $20 or $40 each week and move it to your investment funds. It's a somewhat limited quantity that you perhaps scarcely notice however wind up saving an enormous amount of cash throughout some time.

67 Decide to remain at home as opposed to going out.

Going out will urge you to spend superfluously since you will be enticed to eat at cafés, stop at the corner store, go to the shopping center, and so forth. It is troublesome, and extremely difficult to abstain from spending when you are out and about so remain at home all things being equal and look for other free amusement. You can likewise utilize this available energy to enjoy yourself with your loved ones.

68 Try not to get lists or some other messaged declarations.

This large number of messages and pamphlets are completely planned by organizations to sell you stuff. At the point when you now and again get declarations of cool new items or

 forthcoming deals, creating a buy on extravagance things or service can vary entice. Decide to shut down that large number of index and pamphlet memberships so you don't need to manage to attempt to oppose allurement.

69 Decide to cook at home as opposed to eating out.

This might be hard to do particularly if you are too worn out to even consider cooking following an exhausting day at work. Rather than costly meals or requesting conveyances and takeout cheap food that are not precisely sound, toss in a speedy pan-fried food utilizing new or frozen veggies. You can likewise explore quite a bit early some straightforward and 10-minute recipes, so cooking custom-made and better dishes doesn't need to be a genuine weight.

70 Utilize the envelope framework while isolating your cash.

This is following a similar idea of paying money. Use envelopes to part your discretionary cash flow into the various classes. If you void one envelope, that implies you have spent your allocation.

71 Gain proficiency with the calculation sheet tracker hack.

There are a ton of costly projects out there like Stimulate, MS Cash, and so forth that can assist you with better dealing with your funds. In any case, you don't precisely have to put resources into any of those extravagant programs, particularly on the off chance that you don't have a genuine requirement for every one of the fancy odds and ends that main expense you more. All things considered, you can utilize Google Docs and Calculation sheets, which you can use to monitor your ledger. You can demonstrate dates for each exchange, including titles and sums, alongside a little field for notes or reminders and your running equilibrium.

72 Decide to pay obligation and investment funds first.

Each time you plunk down to go through the entirety of your bills, decide to pay or assign cash first for your reserve funds then, at that point, make your obligation installments. Assuming you continually decide to allot cash for your investment funds for anything that remains, you will oftentimes wind up scamming it. So decide to pay for your reserve funds first. This will assist you with actually scaling back your costs.

73 Dispose of digital television.

Many individuals invest a lot of energy before the TV, a diversion that isn't precisely useful. Rather than spending on link membership, you can decide to download or lease DVDs on the web and just watch the films worth watching and not invest energy filtering pointless shows you find on television more often than not.

74 Decide to utilize online reserve funds rather than conventional bank accounts.

Various web-based banks offer two times as much premium as the typical banks. Be that as it may, you won't get an ATM account or be furnished with a helpful method for pulling out reserves. This obviously can benefit you since you can successfully check the tendency to buy things without much forethought.

75 Decide to track down bliss throughout everyday life and not in spending.

Many individuals decide to purchase stuff thinking subliminally that it will assist them with tracking down enduring bliss. These are the customers who generally want to have the most recent device, the fanciest vehicle, or the most well-known sets of shoes. Honestly, when you purchase stuff, you will be content with your buy for

about a little while probably. From that point forward, you will again want to get some more, which turns into a ceaseless endless loop. All things being equal, decide to adore and appreciate life. You can decide to track down bliss in nature and individuals around you or maybe in doing things that you truly love. There are so many things in life that can give you more bliss, all without the need to spend.

76 Transform your side interest into a productive endeavor.

The possibility of accomplishing something you are very enthusiastic about and creating gain out of it is excessively great of a plan to miss. Assuming you love fiddling with website architecture, sharpen your specialty and consider adapting your inventiveness by taking on logo activities and website composition projects as an afterthought. On the off chance that you love cycling, you can acquire additional pay by fixing and keeping up with bicycles. Individuals who love to eat are making a little fortune selling their manifestations or some very good quality cookware sets.

77 Figure out how to utilize your charge cards intelligently.

Pick the right Mastercard to supplement your ways of managing money so you can take advantage of utilizing Mastercards. Pick cards that give reward focus for buying things that you regularly spend on. So before simply utilizing a card since it's accessible, try to concentrate on what card to best use to buy what.

78 Think about taking part in paid testing.

Turn into a paid analyzer. There are a ton of clinical organizations as well as surface-level engineers that pay analyzers to attempt their medicines and items by and by. To become qualified, you should meet a specific arrangement of prerequisites.

79 Make blood plasma gift.

Obscure to many, blood plasma is a generally highly popular product. The extraordinary thing about making a blood plasma gift is the way that you can really go in and give two times in 7 days, similarly as long as you have no less than 2 in the middle between. You can for the most part get about $20 to $35 for every 16 ounces.

80 Find bringing in cash through reusing.

Attempt to look at it if there are any reusing offices close to your territory. Numerous towns have a few salvaged material reusing offices, which can pay you for each pound of metal you get. What's more, if you live in a state where you are expected to pay a store for each glass bottle, decide to return them to get the store, rather than tossing them out. Notwithstanding, remember that it is against the law to do this across the state lines.

81 Interpretation of a few unspecialized temp jobs.

On the off chance that has the information and aptitude to do fixes, cleanups, or yard work, you can ensure speedy money extending to your administrations for such employment opportunities. If you own a truck, you can offer your administration to pull away trash and bring in serious cash when done consistently.

82 Get an advancement.

On the off chance that you are not exactly agreeable to requesting a compensation raise, the following best thing you can do is procuring that raise by finding a new line of work advancement. It's true that assuming you accomplish more, you are supposed to be paid more. So what about pursuing propelling your vocation and acquiring that advancement? That would mean you want to perform well and do whatever it takes to feature your accomplishments unobtrusively. Be that as it may, you need to check to assume that there is truly space for development in your organization. If an advancement and a compensation raise appear to be far off, you might need to set your sights somewhere else.

83 Sell hand-tailored items on Etsy.

If you have expertise in concocting imaginative things, you can set up a web-based store on Etsy and sell your items. A ton of shoppers these days favor modified and exceptional items - from high-quality wedding welcomes to ornamental pieces, look at a ton of moving Do-It-Yourself thoughts you can cash on at Pinterest.com.

84 Change your insight and demeanor towards cash.

As a business, you are paid with cash to deliver administrations. As a business person, you bring in cash by selling and conveying specific items and administrations. Cash, despite the number of individuals that vibe about it, isn't the foundation, everything being equal. Anyway, it is additionally not the panacea for every one of your torments alongside the world's concerns and ills. Cash is an instrument - - a device that permits you to accomplish a specific way of life that you decide to seek after.

85 Change your opinion of yourself.

You can't characterize your personality in light of running equilibrium or how much cash you procure consistently. In any case, you want to have the attitude that however much you acquire, you are worth the effort. If you accept you are a $30, 000 every year worker, going for $100, 000 is most certainly truly a brain jump. Be prepared to settle on the fundamental vocation and life decisions to improve your capacity to bring in more cash. Rather than "settling" for a task that just offers food of real value, assuming that you are certain you are worth more, you want to make

 the fundamental stages to make something happen and assume better command over your funds.

86 Decide to fabricate your vocation given pay potential.

The fundamental truth is we as a whole work for cash. Furthermore, as you know, there are a few positions than pay more, all without the need to invest additional long periods of backbreaking energy. If your essential inspiration is bringing in more cash, make a point to pick a profession where you can procure more. Put forth your objectives and do whatever it may take to climb the profession stepping stool.

87 Set aside some margin to check your FICO assessment.

Many individuals don't have a clue that one of the quickest ways of saving two or three thousand bucks is to check your financial assessment rating and fix a blunder on your report. By finding an opportunity to further develop your financial assessment, you might save thousands on loan fees consistently.

88 Bring in cash by contributing to a blog.

If you have additional time to burn, contributing to a blog is an extraordinary method for procuring additional pay. While this doesn't give you speedy money, with a while of strong and steady exertion, you can make fair pay. Get everything rolling by getting a pleasant space name and get facilitating administration then set up your blog.

89 Compose item audits.

Various internet-based locales pay you a modest quantity of money by composing item surveys. On the off chance that you compose quick and educated, this might be an extraordinary side occupation for you.

90 Phase homes.

With the developing number of individuals selling houses and managing the very genuine chance of dispossession, you can assist people selling their homes by organizing them for a speedy deal. If you have the energy for configuration, feel free to offer your administrations.

91 Arrangement out your feasts essentially seven days ahead and make your staple rundown in light of the menu plan.

This won't just save you time, stress, and cash, it additionally makes it remarkably simpler to adhere to better eating regimens as opposed to surrendering to fast food and handled items.

92 Stage away from your PC.

The internet-based world has opened up a virtual spot overflowing with interruptions. To expand your efficiency, attempt to do a large portion of your work disconnected.

93 Assuming you are attached to sitting in front of the television, put resources into Tivo.

Consider utilizing DVR or Tivo to successfully chop down one-hour network show down to 40 minutes.

94 Decide to auto-take care of your bills.

By utilizing a mechanized framework, you will save time handling installments and going to installment focuses. Furthermore, you kill those late charges as well as expanded loan costs for missed installments.

95 Learn significant console alternate ways.

Realizing easy routes will save you a lot of time, so attempt to learn more limited console orders, for example, Ctrl +S to save, and so on. This is particularly valuable if your work expects you to work on a PC consistently.

96 Decide to rise and shine prior.

Approaching your tasks while every other person is snoozing and the house is still calm will chop down work in a negligible portion of the time you typically spend. This is an exceptionally commonsense arrangement if you have little kids going around, which makes it extremely difficult to lead a respectable cleanup.

97 Decide to shop online at whatever point it's conceivable.

Rather than going through heaps of apparel, shoes, or some other customer things, by selecting to shop on the web, you can chop down shopping time, gas cost, and check motivation purchasing. This is particularly useful and a viable choice during special times of the year. If you don't precisely savor the prospect of joining another few hundred different customers, then, at that point, do your shopping on the web.

98 Put resources into accelerating your Web by getting broadband association.

Assuming that your work and efficiency significantly depend on your admittance to the web, then it's just possible that you guarantee you have a steady, solid association.

99 Work on further developing your composing speed.

Whether it's composing an email or an article or pretty much whatever other errand that requires encoding, you can save a lot of time by speeding up.

100. Get a Guest ID so you can keep away from those pointless telephone time.

Stay away from calls that are not especially significant and forestall these from diverting you from your work.

End

As you might have determined from the tips given, acquiring more and becoming effective doesn't need to be something incredibly splendid. You don't have to be the innovator to the following best thing set to overturn Facebook. You likewise don't need to be a scientific genius or a big name to fabricate your fortune.

Rather than zeroing in on enormous, aggressive objectives, get some margin to go during that time day's exercises you typically do and find imaginative things to chop down time and set aside cash. Once more, the achievement is the amount of this multitude of little things.

Attempt to adjust useful propensities and a moderate way of life. You needn't bother with that large number of features to display your prosperity or help you have a positive outlook on yourself. Decide to alter, erase and improve your life. Look for compensating things and get rid of exercises that mainly source you to unnecessarily sit around idly and cash.

You will understand that by rolling out little improvements on how you get things done as well as your point of view on life and material stuff, you can eliminate superfluous costs and let loose a greater amount of your time.

The answer to acquiring more is figuring out how to spend less and chasing after your assets. Intentionally decide not to overcomplicate things and stay away from superfluous interruptions that derail your objectives.

Whenever you have dealt with every one of these, you will find the prizes are encouraging.